Book Publishing Log

Kellie Samuels

Book Title:_____

Date Published: ___ /____

Royalty This Month:
Kindle: $_____
Print: $_____
% Change from Last Month: _____
Royalties to Date: $_____

Notes:

_____

_____

_____

_____

_____

_____

_____

_____

_____

_____

_____

_____

_____

_____

Book Title:_____

Date Published: ___/____

Royalty This Month:
Kindle: $_____
Print: $_____
% Change from Last Month: _____
Royalties to Date: $_____

Notes:
_____
_____
_____
_____
_____
_____
_____
_____
_____
_____
_____
_____
_____
_____
_____
_____

Book Title:_____

Date Published: ____/_____

Royalty This Month:
Kindle: $_____
Print: $_____
% Change from Last Month: _____
Royalties to Date: $_____

Notes:
_____
_____
_____
_____
_____
_____
_____
_____
_____
_____
_____
_____
_____
_____
_____
_____
_____

Book Title:_____

Date Published: ___/____

Royalty This Month:
Kindle: $_____
Print: $_____
% Change from Last Month: _____
Royalties to Date: $_____

Notes:
_____
_____
_____
_____
_____
_____
_____
_____
_____
_____
_____
_____
_____
_____
_____
_____
_____

Book Title:_____

Date Published: ___/____

Royalty This Month:
Kindle: $_____
Print: $_____
% Change from Last Month: _____
Royalties to Date: $_____

Notes:
_____
_____
_____
_____
_____
_____
_____
_____
_____
_____
_____
_____
_____
_____
_____

Book Title:_____

Date Published: ___/____

Royalty This Month:
Kindle: $_____
Print: $_____
% Change from Last Month: _____
Royalties to Date: $_____

Notes:
_____
_____
_____
_____
_____
_____
_____
_____
_____
_____
_____
_____
_____
_____
_____
_____

Book Title:_____

Date Published: ___/____

Royalty This Month:
Kindle: $_____
Print: $_____
% Change from Last Month: _____
Royalties to Date: $_____

Notes:
_____
_____
_____
_____
_____
_____
_____
_____
_____
_____
_____
_____
_____
_____

Book Title:_____

Date Published: ____/_____

Royalty This Month:
Kindle: $_____
Print: $_____
% Change from Last Month: _____
Royalties to Date: $_____

Notes:
_____
_____
_____
_____
_____
_____
_____
_____
_____
_____
_____
_____
_____
_____
_____
_____

Book Title:_____

Date Published: ____/_____

Royalty This Month:
Kindle: $_____
Print: $_____
% Change from Last Month: _____
Royalties to Date: $_____

Notes:
_____
_____
_____
_____
_____
_____
_____
_____
_____
_____
_____
_____
_____
_____
_____
_____

Book Title:_____

Date Published: ___/____

Royalty This Month:
Kindle: $_____
Print: $_____
% Change from Last Month: _____
Royalties to Date: $_____

Notes:
_____
_____
_____
_____
_____
_____
_____
_____
_____
_____
_____
_____
_____
_____
_____
_____
_____

Book Title:_____

Date Published: ____/____

Royalty This Month:
Kindle: $_____
Print: $_____
% Change from Last Month: _____
Royalties to Date: $_____

Notes:
_____
_____
_____
_____
_____
_____
_____
_____
_____
_____
_____
_____
_____
_____
_____
_____

Book Title:_____

Date Published: ____/_____

Royalty This Month:
Kindle: $_____
Print: $_____
% Change from Last Month: _____
Royalties to Date: $_____

Notes:
_____
_____
_____
_____
_____
_____
_____
_____
_____
_____
_____
_____
_____
_____
_____
_____

Book Title:_____

Date Published: ___/____

Royalty This Month:
Kindle: $_____
Print: $_____
% Change from Last Month: _____
Royalties to Date: $_____

Notes:
_____
_____
_____
_____
_____
_____
_____
_____
_____
_____
_____
_____
_____
_____
_____
_____
_____

Book Title:_____

Date Published: ___/____

Royalty This Month:
Kindle: $_____
Print: $_____
% Change from Last Month: _____
Royalties to Date: $_____

Notes:
_____
_____
_____
_____
_____
_____
_____
_____
_____
_____
_____
_____
_____
_____
_____
_____
_____
_____

Book Title:_____

Date Published: ____/_____

Royalty This Month:
Kindle: $_____
Print: $_____
% Change from Last Month: _____
Royalties to Date: $_____

Notes:
_____
_____
_____
_____
_____
_____
_____
_____
_____
_____
_____
_____
_____
_____
_____

Book Title:_____

Date Published: ___/____

Royalty This Month:
Kindle: $_____
Print: $_____
% Change from Last Month: _____
Royalties to Date: $_____

Notes:

_____
_____
_____
_____
_____
_____
_____
_____
_____
_____
_____
_____
_____
_____
_____
_____

Book Title:_____

Date Published: ___/____

Royalty This Month:
Kindle: $_____
Print: $_____
% Change from Last Month: _____
Royalties to Date: $_____

Notes:
_____
_____
_____
_____
_____
_____
_____
_____
_____
_____
_____
_____
_____
_____
_____
_____

Book Title:_____

Date Published: ___/____

Royalty This Month:
Kindle: $_____
Print: $_____
% Change from Last Month: _____
Royalties to Date: $_____

Notes:

_____
_____
_____
_____
_____
_____
_____
_____
_____
_____
_____
_____
_____
_____
_____
_____

Book Title:_____

Date Published: ___ /____

Royalty This Month:
Kindle: $_____
Print: $_____
% Change from Last Month: _____
Royalties to Date: $_____

Notes:
_____
_____
_____
_____
_____
_____
_____
_____
_____
_____
_____
_____
_____
_____
_____

Book Title:_____

Date Published: ___/____

Royalty This Month:
Kindle: $_____
Print: $_____
% Change from Last Month: _____
Royalties to Date: $_____

Notes:

_____
_____
_____
_____
_____
_____
_____
_____
_____
_____
_____
_____
_____
_____
_____
_____

Book Title:_____

Date Published: ___ /____

Royalty This Month:
Kindle: $_____
Print: $_____
% Change from Last Month: _____
Royalties to Date: $_____

Notes:
_____
_____
_____
_____
_____
_____
_____
_____
_____
_____
_____
_____
_____
_____
_____

Book Title:_____

Date Published: ____/____

Royalty This Month:
Kindle: $_____
Print: $_____
% Change from Last Month: _____
Royalties to Date: $_____

Notes:

_____
_____
_____
_____
_____
_____
_____
_____
_____
_____
_____
_____
_____
_____
_____
_____

Book Title:_____

Date Published: ___/____

Royalty This Month:
Kindle: $_____
Print: $_____
% Change from Last Month: _____
Royalties to Date: $_____

Notes:
_____
_____
_____
_____
_____
_____
_____
_____
_____
_____
_____
_____
_____
_____
_____

Book Title:_____

Date Published: ___/____

Royalty This Month:
Kindle: $_____
Print: $_____
% Change from Last Month: _____
Royalties to Date: $_____

Notes:
_____
_____
_____
_____
_____
_____
_____
_____
_____
_____
_____
_____
_____
_____
_____
_____

Book Title:_____

Date Published: ___/____

Royalty This Month:
Kindle: $_____
Print: $_____
% Change from Last Month: _____
Royalties to Date: $_____

Notes:
_____
_____
_____
_____
_____
_____
_____
_____
_____
_____
_____
_____
_____
_____
_____
_____
_____

Book Title:_____

Date Published: ____/____

Royalty This Month:
Kindle: $_____
Print: $_____
% Change from Last Month: _____
Royalties to Date: $_____

Notes:
_____
_____
_____
_____
_____
_____
_____
_____
_____
_____
_____
_____
_____
_____
_____
_____
_____

Book Title:_____

Date Published: ___/____

Royalty This Month:
Kindle: $_____
Print: $_____
% Change from Last Month: _____
Royalties to Date: $_____

Notes:
_____
_____
_____
_____
_____
_____
_____
_____
_____
_____
_____
_____
_____
_____
_____
_____

Book Title:_____

Date Published: ___/____

Royalty This Month:
Kindle: $_____
Print: $_____
% Change from Last Month: _____
Royalties to Date: $_____

Notes:
_____
_____
_____
_____
_____
_____
_____
_____
_____
_____
_____
_____
_____
_____
_____
_____

Book Title:_____

Date Published: ___/____

Royalty This Month:
Kindle: $_____
Print: $_____
% Change from Last Month: _____
Royalties to Date: $_____

Notes:
_____
_____
_____
_____
_____
_____
_____
_____
_____
_____
_____
_____
_____
_____
_____
_____

Book Title:_____

Date Published: ___/____

Royalty This Month:
Kindle: $_____
Print: $_____
% Change from Last Month: _____
Royalties to Date: $_____

Notes:
_____
_____
_____
_____
_____
_____
_____
_____
_____
_____
_____
_____
_____
_____
_____
_____

www.ingramcontent.com/pod-product-compliance
Lightning Source LLC
Chambersburg PA
CBHW030912180526
45163CB00004B/1802